DEPORTATION

CATHLEEN SMALL

Published in 2018 by
Lucent Press, an Imprint of Greenhaven Publishing, LLC
353 3rd Avenue
Suite 255
New York, NY 10010

Produced for Lucent by Calcium
Designer: Jeni Child
Picture researcher: Rachel Blount
Editors: Sarah Eason and Nancy Dickmann

Picture credits: Cover: Shutterstock: Vinokurov Kirill (top), Mark Scott Spatny (main); Inside: Shutterstock: Alexandre17 26, Antoniodiaz 37, Anthony Correia 57, Danielfela 40, Evan El-Amin 13, 53, ESB Professional 44, Everett Historical 14–15, 16, 17, 18–19, 20t, 20–21b, 22, 23, Blaj Gabriel 47t, Gila Photography 24, Glazok90 45, Thomas Koch 49, Bill Lawson 50–51, David Litman 55, Merzzie 47b, Christopher Penler 61, Alexander Raths 11b, Rawpixel.com 30–31, Rena Schild 28–29, 48, Joseph Sohm 32, Ken Tannenbaum 12, Melih Cevdet Teksen 41, Wavebreakmedia 36–37, 39, Chad Zuber 42–43; Wikimedia Commons: 8, Russell Lee, Farm Security Administration—Office of War Information Photograph Collection, Library of Congress 7, Alfred, Jacob Miller/Walter's Art Museum 4–5, National Park Service, U.S. Dept. of the Interior 11t, Gerald L. Nino, CBP, U.S. Dept. of Homeland Security 35, Aaron Tang 58–59, James Anthony Wills 9.

Cataloging-in-Publication Data

Names: Small, Cathleen.
Title: Deportation / Cathleen Small.
Description: New York : Lucent Press, 2018. | Series: Crossing the border | Includes index.
Identifiers: ISBN 9781534562257 (library bound) | ISBN 9781534562264 (ebook) | ISBN 9781534562776 (paperback)
Subjects: LCSH: Illegal aliens–United States–Juvenile literature. | Illegal aliens–Government policy–United States–Juvenile literature. | Immigrants–United States–Juvenile literature.
Classification: LCC JV6483.S63 2018 | DDC 364.1'37–dc23

Printed in the United States of America

CPSIA compliance information: Batch #CW18KL: For further information contact Greenhaven Publishing LLC, New York, New York at 1-844-317-7404.

Please visit our website, www.greenhavenpublishing.com. For a free color catalog of all our high-quality books, call toll free 1-844-317-7404 or fax 1-844-317-7405.

CONTENTS

CHAPTER 1

THE HISTORY OF DEPORTATION

Wherever there is citizenship, there will naturally also be noncitizens. People who are living in a country where they do not hold citizenship can be deported and sent back to the country where they are citizens. But they are not the only ones who face deportation. Over the long history of the United States, many noncitizens have been deported, but United States citizens with ancestry in other countries have also faced deportation.

AMERICANS: THE ORIGINAL UNDOCUMENTED IMMIGRANTS?

Some people argue that the first immigrants to come to North America illegally were the colonists, since they came from Europe and took land from the Native Americans. But others disagree, saying that Native Americans did not own land and had no centralized formal government—they resided in North America, but anyone could reside there at that point.

It's an argument that is tough to answer. However, for legal purposes, most would say the first immigrants that technically came illegally did so after the first immigration laws were put in place. Interestingly enough, some of the earliest ones to immigrate illegally were actually Americans trying to move into what, at the time, was Mexico's territory.

Long before the colonists arrived from Europe, groups of Native Americans populated North America.

THE STORY OF TEXAS

Modern-day Texas is now an important part of the United States, but in the early 1800s it belonged to Spain. In 1821, Mexico won independence from Spain, and much of the territory that is now Texas became part of Mexico, called Mexican Texas.

At first, Mexico allowed U.S. citizens to immigrate to Mexican Texas. However, by 1834 there were nearly four times as many white settlers in the region as Mexican residents. Mexican authorities could see a potential problem developing, if they were outnumbered so heavily. They banned nearly all immigration from the United States in 1830, but that didn't stop some persistent settlers.

In 1830, a Mexican army officer named Colonel José de las Piedras reported that American citizens were trying to enter Mexican Texas near what is now Houston. He ordered them to leave the region, because they had no passports, but they talked him into letting them stay for 20 days to attend to business.

The American immigrants stayed and moved farther into Texas, enraging Colonel Piedras. He wrote, "As they have come into this country contrary to law and have disrespected the authorities, I think they ought not to be admitted."

TERMINOLOGY

Undocumented immigrant, illegal alien, illegal immigrant, and unauthorized immigrant are all terms you may have heard, but what do they all mean? These terms all refer to someone living without authorization in a country that is not their country of citizenship. How they arrived in that country may vary, and the reasons why they're undocumented may vary too. But the end result is the same: it is a person living without authorization in a country other than the one in which they hold citizenship.

Some people feel that the term "illegal immigrant" implies that the person has done something criminal. In reality, most undocumented immigrants have no criminal history and are simply living in the United States without authorization.

A CHANGING SITUATION

Since those early days, the situation has reversed. In the mid-nineteenth century, Americans were the ones pushing illegally into Texas. Today Mexican immigrants have long made up the biggest portion of the undocumented immigrant population in the United States.

At times, the U.S. government has been more or less accepting of this. They know that Mexican laborers contribute to the American economy when they accept agricultural and service-industry jobs that American citizens aren't as likely to fill. But at times, suspicion and unrest among American citizens have led to worries about immigrants—and sometimes even mass deportations.

Mothers like this one with her children were deported during the Great Depression, when jobs were scarce for U.S. citizens.

DEPRESSION-ERA MASS DEPORTATION

One series of mass deportations took place in the 1930s and into the 1940s. During the 1930s, the Great Depression swept across the United States, leaving many people unemployed. Many American citizens worried that Mexicans were taking all the jobs. So governments created so-called repatriation campaigns, in which they would raid workplaces and public events and round up people of Mexican descent for deportation.

In the raids, government officials would pressure Mexicans and Mexican-Americans to leave the United States voluntarily. In Los Angeles, for example, social workers told Mexican-Americans receiving public assistance that they were going to lose their assistance and they should go to Mexico. The social workers would even provide tickets for the families to travel back to Mexico. In this way, a third of Los Angeles' Mexican population left for Mexico between 1929 and 1944.

DEPORTING CITIZENS?

In total, approximately 2 million Mexicans and Mexican-Americans were deported under the campaigns of the 1930s and 1940s. Historians estimate that more than half of the deportees were actually United States citizens of Mexican descent. They were people who were born in the United States, making them natural-born citizens who had lived in the United States for their entire lives.

WORKING TOGETHER

During the 1920s, more than 62,000 Mexicans had been entering the United States by legal means each year, and more than 100,000 were crossing the border without documentation each year. And it wasn't just the U.S. government that was concerned about the number of undocumented Mexican immigrants entering the United States—the Mexican government was worried too. So many laborers had left Mexico for the United States that Mexico's own agricultural economy was suffering. Crops rotted in the fields because there weren't enough laborers left to harvest them.

To address the problem, the Mexican and U.S. governments worked together to establish the Bracero Program. Under this program, the Mexican government agreed to allow Mexican laborers to enter the United States on short-term contracts to work in the fields. In exchange, the United States would provide wages, housing, and food to the laborers, and would also crack down on undocumented immigrants coming into the United States.

Housing for people in the Bracero Program was often very basic.

This program was not fully enforced. Some farmers provided fair wages, housing, and food to Mexican laborers, and others didn't. And in some people's view, the United States did not effectively control the flow of undocumented immigrants moving from Mexico to the United States. Even when the United States did deport Mexicans living without documentation in the United States, many of them simply reentered at a later time.

OPERATION WETBACK

This situation created considerable tension between the Mexican and United States governments. The solution created by both governments in 1954 was called Operation Wetback. "Wetback" is a derogatory and offensive term for a Mexican laborer—it comes from the days when undocumented immigrants would swim across the Rio Grande to cross the border into Texas. It is a slur and is not an acceptable term to use today. However, it was part of the official operation name.

President Dwight Eisenhower appointed General Joseph Swing to head up the operation. He would be working alongside a former government agency called Immigration and Naturalization Service. Responsibility controlling immigration is now divided among three agencies under the Department of Homeland Security.

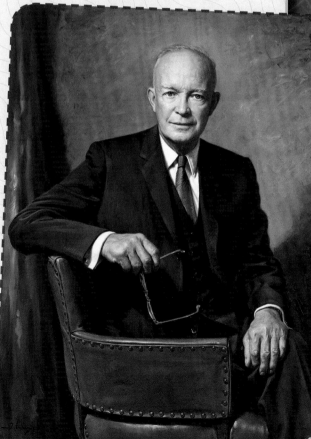

Dwight D. Eisenhower was the presidential face behind the operation. »

9

How It Worked

At the start of the operation, the United States established a large team of immigration and border patrol officers. The officers were dispatched to the United States–Mexico border region to track down, process, and deport undocumented Mexican immigrants. They handed the deportees to Mexican officials who, instead of sending them to their home city in Mexico, sent them deep into central and southern Mexico, where there were job opportunities. The idea was that if they were sent somewhere with jobs available, they would be less likely to try to enter the United States illegally again.

In its first year, the operation apprehended and deported more than a million undocumented Mexican immigrants. Many more undocumented immigrants voluntarily fled home to Mexico because they feared being arrested under the operation.

Problems Arise

The operation was not exactly a success, because it brought about serious human rights violations. When the officers located undocumented immigrants, they often deported them without even allowing them to contact their families or recover their belongings. It left many stranded in the brutal summer heat in Mexico, without food, employment, or money. In July 1955 alone, 88 deportees died in the heat.

Another problem was that some of the deportees made their way back to the border and reentered the United States. When they were caught again, U.S. Border Patrol agents would reportedly shave their heads to mark them as repeat offenders. Sometimes, they would also beat and jail them before deporting them for a second time. Many deportees were too frightened to report this abuse, but some spoke out. In the ten-year span from 1954 to 1964, there were 11,000 formal complaints made by deportees.

U.S. President Lyndon B. Johnson and Mexican President Adolfo López Mateos unveiled a new border marker in 1964.

THE ANTI-DRUG ABUSE ACT

This style of mass deportation may be hard to imagine today, but the reality is that it's still happening. In the late 1980s and 1990s, Congress responded to widespread fear that immigrants were creating an unsafe atmosphere in the United States. They passed several laws that increased the number of immigrants who could be deported. The first was the Anti-Drug Abuse Act of 1988, which made a number of drug-related crimes aggravated felonies. This meant that any immigrant found guilty of these crimes was subject to immediate deportation.

Depending on the crime, an undocumented immigrant may be deported immediately.

MODERN-DAY MASS DEPORTATIONS

In 1996, Congress passed the Anti-Terrorism and Effective Death Penalty Act and the Illegal Immigration Reform and Responsibility Act. Both of these laws turned certain nonviolent misdemeanor crimes, including shoplifting and drug possession, into deportable offenses. These acts also redefined what "conviction" meant in terms of deportation. Under the new laws, even if a judge ruled for probation in a criminal sense, the individual convicted of the crime could still be deported.

These reforms also made immigrants subject to immediate deportation if they had any record of these crimes in their past—in other words, their past crimes could come back to haunt them, even if they were currently living a law-abiding life.

DEPORTATION IN A POST-9/11 WORLD

When the United States was hit by devastating terrorist attacks on September 11, 2001, national security suddenly became a much bigger issue for many people. Fear of immigrants became even more pronounced. The United States government instituted numerous policies after 9/11 that have resulted in a steady increase in the rate of deportation. For example, the PATRIOT Act, enacted in 2001 right after the 9/11 attacks, allowed for the deportation of any immigrant known to have any association with what the government considered a terrorist group, even without evidence of specific terrorist acts.

The 9/11 attacks changed the face of immigration and deportation in the United States.

The act's effect on deportation was striking. In 2013 the United States deported 438,421 immigrants, which is more than double the number of immigrants deported in 2003. Astonishingly, the 2013 deportation is almost nine times the number in the early- to mid-1990s, when fewer than 50,000 immigrants were deported each year. That number had jumped to more than 100,000 deportees by 1997, and it increased to about 211,000 deportees in 2003, under the newly formed Department of Homeland Security.

Obama's Policy

Under President Barack Obama, who was elected in 2008, the government was reasonably welcoming to immigrants and refugees. In fact, that was one of Donald Trump's arguing points

 President Obama's administration deported many people who were living in the country without documentation.

during his 2016 presidential campaign—that he would tighten immigration and focus heavily on deporting undocumented immigrants, which were things he felt Obama had failed to do. But in reality, the United States deported more immigrants under the Obama administration than under any other president in United States history; however, many claim this is largely due to a shift in what deportation is now considered to mean.

CHAPTER 2

THE HISTORY OF IMMIGRATION LAWS

To understand the current system, it's useful to understand the long and complex history of immigration laws in the United States. The country's first official deportation laws were the Alien and Sedition Acts, passed in 1798. These acts were made up of four separate bills, and two of them addressed deportation. The Alien Friends Act of 1798 mandated that the president could imprison and deport immigrants he found to be dangerous.

The Alien Enemy Act of 1798 was similar, except it stated that the president could imprison or deport anyone from a nation deemed hostile to the United States. The Alien Friends Act was repealed a few short years later, under President Thomas Jefferson. However, the Alien Enemy Act actually remains in effect today, although it has been revised significantly.

Slaves like the ones depicted in this drawing were safe from deportation, but they had an incredibly hard life.

SLAVERY IN THE UNITED STATES

In the early days of the United States, slavery was common, particularly in the South. At the time, the economy was actually reliant on slave labor. A large amount of the work slaves were forced to do was agricultural work which was most cheaply done with slave labor.

However, in 1808, the Act Prohibiting Importation of Slaves went into effect, stating that no new slaves could be brought into the United States. The slave trade was still allowed within the United States, so this act didn't end slavery—it simply made it illegal to import new slaves from outside the country.

SLAVERY AND DEPORTATION

Slaves were not usually subject to deportation, because even after the 1808 law, they were still considered property. Only people living in the United States illegally could be deported—and although it is horrible, slaves were essentially considered property, not people, so they didn't qualify.

After the Civil War ended in 1865, the Thirteenth Amendment to the Constitution outlawed slavery and gave slaves the right to pursue citizenship. However, having the right to pursue citizenship didn't necessarily mean it would be granted. After the slaves were freed by the signing of the Emancipation Proclamation in 1863, some U.S. politicians felt they shouldn't be allowed to live among white Americans. Some thought a solution was to send the freed black slaves to British colonies in the Caribbean. This plan was known as colonization.

CHILDREN OF SLAVES

One group of African Americans who didn't have to worry about deportation was children born to slaves who had been brought into the country. The Civil Rights Act of 1866 ruled that all children born to these slaves were automatically granted U.S. citizenship. However, they didn't necessarily get all of the rights and privileges of a U.S. citizen—many still suffered from harsh discrimination.

FAMOUS FACES

ABRAHAM LINCOLN

One politician who seemed to have supported a plan of colonization was the man credited with freeing the slaves—President Abraham Lincoln. Lincoln signed the Emancipation Proclamation in January 1863, but documents found in the National Archives dating from later in the same year show Lincoln authorizing a British colonial agent named John Hodge to recruit freed slaves to be sent to colonies. These colonies were in modern-day Guyana and Belize. Lincoln reportedly also considered sending freed slaves to Panama to work on building a canal.

However, the colonization plans never happened. Congress voted against them. In addition, the British did not support them—they feared that if the Confederacy were to win the Civil War, they would reverse emancipation. If that happened, British agents who had recruited freed slaves could be considered thieves, because the Confederacy viewed slaves as property.

Some historians believe that Lincoln continued to pursue the idea of colonization with freed black slaves, even after Congress voted it down. A letter sent to Lincoln by his Attorney General just months before Lincoln was assassinated indicates that Lincoln was still exploring the idea.

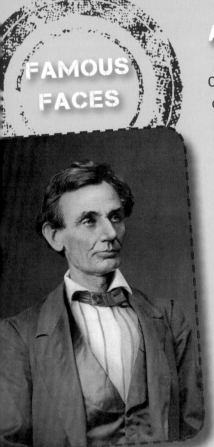

Abraham Lincoln may have freed the slaves, but he also considered sending them out of the country.

Asian Immigration

Another group of immigrants was treated with racism and outright hostility, much as the freed slaves had been. They were immigrants from Asia. Chinese immigrants arrived in large numbers during the Gold Rush in the 1850s and to work on the Transcontinental Railroad. Japanese immigrants began arriving in the United States in the late 1860s.

Many of the Japanese immigrants settled in Hawaii to work in the sugar cane fields. While their lives weren't exactly easy—many worked and lived in harsh conditions that were essentially indentured servitude—they came to be generally accepted. So many Japanese immigrants came to Hawaii that they made up a significant chunk of the islands' population, and thus they weren't seen so much as outsiders.

 This 1857 image depicts the Asian immigrants who came to the western United States to work during the Gold Rush.

XENOPHOBIA

Some Japanese immigrants came to the West Coast of the United States—either directly from Japan or from Hawaii. Some of them were fleeing their indentured servitude contracts. Many Chinese immigrants had settled on the West Coast, too, but neither ethnic group was represented in large numbers. In fact, they made up quite a small percentage of the population in the region.

Due to their minority status, Chinese and Japanese immigrants were seen as outsiders. Xenophobia was strong, and white Americans were suspicious of everything about the Asian newcomers. To many, they looked different, sounded different, and had a completely different culture. The United States may have billed itself as a "melting pot" and a place for immigrants to find a home, but natural-born U.S. citizens were notoriously skeptical of newcomers.

THE PAGE ACT

The government took steps to limit Asian immigration in 1875, when Congress passed the Page Act. The act specifically banned Asian immigrants from coming to the United States for the purpose of working in forced labor. Because forced labor was many Asian immigrants' ticket to the United States, the Page Act severely limited the number of Asian immigrants who were able to come to America.

The Page Act also made it particularly difficult for Asian women to come to the United States. Certain provisions particularly made it so essentially no Chinese woman could come into the country without great difficulty.

The majority of Asian immigrants were men, but some women did manage to immigrate as well.

THE CHINESE EXCLUSION ACT

In 1882, Congress further limited Asian immigration by passing the Chinese Exclusion Act, which prohibited nearly all immigration from China. This act didn't force the deportation of Chinese people who were already in the United States, but it did result in somewhat of a voluntary deportation. Some Chinese immigrants returned to China when the law was passed and they realized they wouldn't be able to bring their families over to join them. The act also made travel back to China difficult for the Chinese immigrants. If they left the United States, they had to get a certification to reenter. If they wanted to be certain to be allowed to stay in the United States, it was generally best just not to leave. Indeed, by 1888 the Scott Act had passed, which prohibited Chinese immigrants from reentering the United States if they left it.

THE GEARY ACT

In 1892, Congress passed the Geary Act, which required Chinese immigrants to register and carry a certificate of residence. Without a certificate, they could be arrested, given a year of hard labor, and then deported. Not surprisingly, many Chinese immigrants resisted and refused to register. In fact, only about 14 percent of Chinese immigrants registered. Low registration numbers meant there were about 85,000 unregistered Chinese immigrants for the government to arrest and deport. This would have cost approximately $7 million, but they had only budgeted $60,000. Congress eventually had to pass an amendment that allowed Chinese immigrants an additional six months to register.

Although many Chinese immigrants came to the west coast, there were also settlements in the east, such as New York's Chinatown.

NEW TERMS FOR JAPANESE IMMIGRANTS

Congress threatened to pass a Japanese Exclusion Act, similar to the Chinese Exclusion Act, but instead came to an agreement with the Japanese government in 1908. The Japanese would limit the number of their own citizens emigrating to the United States, and in exchange the United States would allow immediate family members of Japanese residing in the country to come over.

DENIED CITIZENSHIP

Many Asian immigrants had settled in California, and in 1913 the state passed the California Alien Land Law. This made all undocumented immigrants ineligible for land ownership and citizenship. The law was written with the intent of discouraging Chinese, Indian, Korean, and especially Japanese immigrants from coming to California. The law had an indirect effect on deportation. If Asian immigrants couldn't become naturalized citizens, they would continue to be subject to deportation if any of their actions warranted their removal.

Immigration laws for Asians were incredibly strict, but the Immigration Act of 1917 tightened them further. It designated an "Asiatic Barred Zone" that included much of Asia and the Pacific Islands. No one could immigrate to the United States from this zone. However, the zone did not include Japan and the Philippines, so immigrants could still come from there. The Philippines were a U.S. colony, and Japanese immigration had already been limited by the agreement with the Japanese government.

The Immigration Act of 1924 established immigration quotas for many countries, but it completely banned Asian immigrants. This time, even the Japanese were banned. The act stated that any person ineligible for citizenship could not immigrate to the United States. Since the Japanese were ineligible for citizenship at that time, they could not come.

Many Japanese immigrants found work on Hawaiian plantations.

JAPANESE INTERNMENT

After the Japanese attacked a U.S. naval base at Pearl Harbor, Hawaii, the United States declared war on Japan. Soon after that, President Franklin D. Roosevelt signed Executive Order 9066, also known as the Japanese Internment Order. In the spring of 1942, all immigrants of Japanese descent were ordered to collect their necessary belongings and report to control centers. At these control centers, more than 100,000 Japanese immigrants were sent to internment camps located in California, Arizona, Utah, Idaho, Colorado, and Wyoming.

At the Manzanar Relocation Center in California, Japanese women worked as seamstresses.

This wasn't deportation in the strictest sense—the Japanese weren't required to leave the country. However, it was a forced relocation. The immigrants had to give up most of their assets, and anything they sold was generally bought at only a fraction of its value, so they were left with very little to show for their years of work in the United States.

The camps consisted of barracks covered in tar paper and communal dining halls. Adults could work for a small salary if they wanted, and there were some activities for people to pass the time. These camps were not like the concentration camps in Europe, where people were starved and killed. But the barracks were primitive, the food was basic and not terribly tasty, and people were not allowed to leave—if they tried, guards would shoot them.

RELAXING THE RESTRICTIONS

Despite the internment of the Japanese, restrictions of immigration from Asia eased up a bit in 1943. The Magnuson Act (also known as the Chinese Exclusion Repeal Act) allowed some Chinese immigrants already living in the United States to apply for citizenship. It also allowed an annual quota of 105 immigrants to enter the United States from China. However, in many states, Chinese immigrants still could not own property.

Another internment camp, the Granada War Relocation Center, was located in Colorado.

The Immigration and Nationality Act of 1965 further relaxed the rules on Asian immigration. It abolished the practice of using race, ancestry, or national origin as criteria for determining immigration eligibility. People could no longer be denied entry into the United States simply because they were from Africa or Asia. In addition, immediate family of U.S. citizens were no longer subject to immigration quotas and were given immigration priority.

Immigration laws have continued to change since 1965, but current laws do not discriminate against Asian immigrants in the same way that previous laws did. Now, Asians are subject to immigration quotas just like people from any other part of the world.

Often an immigrant's greatest fear is deportation. Most immigrants try to live quiet, law-abiding lives so that they won't be brought to the attention of immigration authorities who could potentially deport them.

Most immigrants come to the United States to make a better life for themselves. If they are deported, they may be going back to a life of poverty or difficult conditions. For some immigrants, such as refugees and asylees, they could be returning to a potentially dangerous or deadly situation. And some immigrants came to the United States at such a young age that they've never known a life in another country, and they have no ties in their home country.

This warning sign is riddled with bullet holes, evidence of the danger that some immigrants face.

TRAVEL CAUTION
SMUGGLING AND ILLEGAL IMMIGRATION MAY BE ENCOUNTERED IN THIS AREA

Esteban Torres was born in the United States and thus has always been an American citizen. He was three years old when his father was deported in 1933 during a repatriation campaign at a copper mine where he worked in Arizona. His father, who was a U.S. citizen of Mexican descent, was not given a chance to say goodbye to his family before being deported. Torres remembers, "My mother, like other wives, waited for the husbands to come home from the mine. But he didn't come home. I was three years old. My brother was two years old. And we never saw my father again."

Torres' father had been active in efforts to organize miners in a union, and Torres' mother suspected that was why he had been rounded up and deported. That childhood experience and his father's legacy led Torres to devote his life to causes of organized labor. He was elected to the United States House of Representatives in 1983 and served as a representative for 16 years.

WHO CAN BE DEPORTED?

The most obvious candidates for deportation are undocumented immigrants. They are living in the country illegally, and thus they are subject to deportation. But unless there are extenuating circumstances, they are granted a hearing first. They are not immediately deported simply for living in the United States without documentation.

A person might be living in the United States without documentation because they crossed the border illegally, or they might have entered under a legitimate temporary visa that has since expired. Either way, they are considered undocumented and thus are subject to the deportation process.

REASONS FOR DEPORTATION

Other immigrants are subject to deportation, too, though. In fact, any immigrant who violates the terms of their stay is subject to deportation. There are a number of common violations for which a non-U.S. citizen can be deported. For example, some people enter the United States as a nonimmigrant. This means that they do not intend to stay permanently in the country. An example of this is a person who enters on a travel visa. In doing so, they must agree to various conditions, such as not working while in the United States. If they accept a job, they can be deported.

Immigrants must keep their paperwork up to date. They have ten days to notify U.S. Citizenship and Immigration Services of a change of address. If they fail to meet this requirement, it's actually considered to be a criminal offense, and they can be deported.

Establishing residency requires a lot of paperwork that can result in deportation if not kept up to date.

Committing a Crime

Many immigrants are deported for committing a crime. Not all crimes are deportable offenses, but many are. Human trafficking, weapons trafficking, document fraud, drug offenses, money laundering, espionage, sabotage, terrorism, murder, and other aggravated felonies are all deportable offenses. Undocumented immigrants, nonimmigrants, and green card holders alike can be deported if they commit any of these crimes. In addition, so-called crimes of moral turpitude are deportable offenses, as is domestic violence.

Even if a state or local authority labels a particular crime simply a misdemeanor, immigration authorities step in. They can make a different decision about how the crime is classified for the purposes of immigration law and deportation.

» EMILIA

PERSONAL STORIES

Emilia was born in Los Angeles in 1926, making her an American citizen. Her parents were Mexican immigrants. Emilia's mother died when she was young, and in 1935 Los Angeles County rounded up Emilia and her father in a repatriation campaign and put them on a train to Mexico. They ended up living with extended family in Mexico but often sleeping outside because there was no room inside with them.

Emilia remembers her Mexican relatives calling her a *repatriada*, or repatriate. "I don't think I felt that I was a *repatriada*, because I was an American citizen," she remembered. It was a confusing time for Emilia, who finally returned to the United States when she was 17, leaving her father behind in Mexico.

VIOLATING IMMIGRATION LAWS

A person who violates immigration law can also be deported. Examples of this would be participating in a fraudulent marriage for the purposes of citizenship, or helping to smuggle other unauthorized immigrants into the United States. Smugglers bring people over the border from Mexico without documentation in return for payment. If caught, they could be charged with violation of immigration laws and deported.

PUBLIC ASSISTANCE

To get a green card, an immigrant must promise to support him or herself and not become a financial burden on society. If an immigrant relies on government assistance within the first five years of entering the United States on a green card, he or she is considered to be a "public charge" and can be deported. If the immigrant has a green card, though, there are ways to avoid deportation in this instance. They can ask their petitioner or sponsor to provide financial support, and they can reimburse any public agencies from which they received assistance. Those steps may keep them from getting deported.

Children of Immigrants

Some immigrants do not have legal resident or immigration status because they were brought illegally into the United States as a child and have remained undocumented ever since. If that's the case and they are faced with deportation, they may be able to request a two-year delay in deportation.

In 2012, a program called Deferred Action for Childhood Arrivals (DACA) was created. Under the program, these immigrants could request the two-year deferral. If the request was granted, they could stay in the United States for two years and obtain a work permit. In 2017, President Trump moved to end DACA, bringing much concern and uncertainty about the future of the program.

The DACA program was created to deal with the issue of children who had been brought into the country without documentation by immigrant parents. Essentially, it didn't seem fair to deport undocumented immigrants who had not made their own choice to come to the country. Their parents had made the decision and brought them. Many of these children had grown up going to United States schools, speaking fluent English, and largely assimilating to American culture. Deporting them to a home country that many couldn't remember and possibly had no ties remaining in brought up serious ethical concerns. The DACA program was created to address these concerns.

People marched to show their support of the DACA program outside the Supreme Court in 2016.

›› YVES

Yves was brought to the United States as a toddler in 1994. His parents sought asylum, and while their case was being reviewed they were allowed to work. Their asylum case took 12 years to review, and in that time Yves grew up in Maryland, going to schools and making friends. His mother taught at a community college and worked on a PhD. His father was a server at a large hotel in Washington, D.C.

In 2006, the government finally denied the family's asylum. As undocumented citizens no longer awaiting asylum, Yves' parents were no longer allowed to work. In 2008, Yves' father got pulled over for a broken taillight. When the officer discovered he was undocumented, he reported it to Immigration and Customs Enforcement. Immigration officers raided the family's home and deported Yves' father back to Bangladesh. His mother was allowed to stay for a year to settle her affairs before being deported back to India. However, she had to wear an electronic tracking device on her ankle.

Yves and his brother were allowed to stay in the United States temporarily under the DACA program. Even though he was an excellent student, Yves found getting an education difficult because of his status. Ultimately, he earned a bachelor's degree in biochemistry, but he is unsure he will be allowed to remain in the country where he has lived since he was a toddler.

DACA Rules

The DACA program came with strict rules controlling eligibility. Most of them reference a person's status as of June 15, 2012—the date that the act was implemented. For example, to request DACA, a person had to be between the ages of 15 and 31 as of that date.

In addition, an applicant must have come to the United States before the age of 16, and must have resided there continuously since June 15, 2007. They must have been physically present in the United States on June 15, 2012, with no lawful status as of that date.

DACA was designed to help undocumented immigrants who have been good citizens. Because of that, an applicant could not have been convicted of a felony, a significant misdemeanor, or three less serious misdemeanors. If they're not in school, they must have obtained a high school diploma or GED, or been honorably discharged from the armed forces or the Coast Guard.

DACA was created as a way for students whose parents were undocumented immigrants to remain in the United States to finish their education.

APPLYING FOR DACA

Immigrants who have applied to stay in the United States under DACA faced a complicated process. When an immigrant requested DACA, they had to collect many different types of documentation to support their application. This included official proof of identity, proof that they came to the United States before the age of 16, proof of immigration status, proof of presence in the United States on June 15, 2012, proof that they have continuously resided in the United States since June 15, 2007, and either proof of student status at the time of requesting DACA or proof of an honorable discharge from the armed forces.

After gathering all the documentation, completing the required forms, and submitting the packet to U.S. Citizenship and Immigration Services, the immigrant applying for DACA would visit an Application Support Center for a biometrics appointment. At this appointment they would be fingerprinted and photographed. Their fingerprints and photographs were then submitted to the FBI for clearance.

Proof of service in the U.S. armed forces could serve as support for a DACA application.

DACA FEES

Applying for DACA could be expensive as well as time-consuming. The biometrics appointment and the application fee together cost nearly $500. Certain fee exemptions were made available for applicants who fell into one of several categories.

Applicants under 18 years old with an income less than 150 percent of the U.S. poverty level, and in foster care or otherwise lacking parental support, could be granted an exemption. Disabled applicants with a low income could also be eligible. A third category could cover applicants who have accumulated at least $10,000 in medical debt over the past 12 months (either for their own care or for that of an immediate family member), and who met the low income requirements.

MAKING A DECISION

If U.S. Citizenship and Immigration Services granted DACA, they would send a written notice of the decision. They would also send an Employment Authorization Document so the person may obtain employment. Successful applicants still have to be careful with traveling outside of the United States under DACA. Failure to obtain advance permission to do so can affect their continuous resident status and can result in their DACA being revoked. The decision of U.S. Citizenship and Immigration Services to grant or not grant DACA to an individual is final. The person cannot appeal the decision.

CHAPTER 4

THE DEPORTATION PROCESS

Identifying and finding an undocumented immigrant is just the start of the process that may lead to deportation. When officials from Immigration and Customs Enforcement (ICE) identify an undocumented immigrant and act upon it, a few things can happen.

The ICE officials may arrest the immigrant at home or in his or her workplace. By law, immigrants do not have to let officers into their home if they don't have a warrant, but many don't know this. Also, the people who perform the arrest may not work for ICE. Sometimes state or local police will arrest the person for a minor criminal act or a traffic violation, and the immigrant will then be turned over to ICE. U.S. Customs and Border Patrol officers can also arrest undocumented immigrants.

TIME LIMIT

If another member of law enforcement arrests an undocumented immigrant, they cannot simply hold the immigrant indefinitely while they wait for ICE to come interview the person. ICE can file a detainer to have the immigrant held for a maximum of 48 hours. If they are not able to interview the immigrant within 48 hours, the immigrant must be released.

DIFFERENT RIGHTS

Undocumented immigrants do not always get treated with the same rights as U.S. citizens when they are arrested. For example, undocumented immigrants are not always protected from unreasonable search and seizure, read their Miranda rights, or given a trial by jury.

All of these are constitutional rights, but the catch is that they apply to criminal proceedings, and deportation is considered an administrative proceeding. That means officials may search an undocumented immigrant's home or workplace without a warrant. The immigrant has the right to an immigration hearing, but it is a hearing in front of a judge—not in front of a jury of his or her peers.

Miranda rights inform people who are arrested that they have the right to remain silent, that anything they say can be used against them in court, and that they have the right to an attorney, even if the person cannot afford one. Even if an officer doesn't read these rights aloud to an undocumented immigrant, they still apply. However, some immigrants—particularly those who face a language barrier—may not be aware of those rights, which could be helpful to know during their deportment proceedings.

A customs officer reads someone their rights.

AINEE

PERSONAL STORIES

Ainee and her mother arrived in the United States in the 1990s when Ainee was two years old. They came from Pakistan so that Ainee could receive high-quality treatment for leukemia. While Ainee was being treated, her father was offered an employment visa, and the company sponsoring him applied for a visa for their entire family. After years of waiting, the family found out the visa had been denied.

They then applied for asylum based on religious persecution, because Ahmadi Muslims were not safe in Pakistan. By this time, Ainee was attending the University of Texas-Austin. A judge rejected their asylum case, but the family appealed. During Ainee's sophomore year at UT-Austin, ICE officials raided her family's home in Houston and took her parents to a detention center. The attorney they had hired for their asylum appeal had never filed the paperwork, so they were living in the United States undocumented.

After a month, Ainee's parents were released, but they had to wear monitoring bracelets on their ankles for six months, and Ainee and her sister were monitored under the Intensive Supervision Appearance Program. As part of the program, they would receive periodic phone calls from ICE, and if they didn't answer them within three rings, the immigration officers would be alerted. Although Ainee did finish her education at UT-Austin, she found it hard to fully participate while under constant supervision and monitoring.

Ainee and her family were allowed to stay in the United States while she finished her education under the DACA program, for which Ainee is grateful. However, she longs for a real path to citizenship, so she doesn't have to leave the only home she can remember and so that she can work in the United States.

Immigration Lawyers

It is clear that an immigrant detained for potential deportation isn't always treated with the same rights as a person detained for a criminal offense—regardless of whether the immigrant is actually a documented immigrant or an undocumented one.

However, the immigrant always has the right to an immigration lawyer. For immigration hearings, the lawyer will normally charge an hourly fee, which can get quite costly depending on the complexity of the case and how many hours the lawyer puts in. So while the immigrant has the right to a lawyer, whether he or she will actually be able to afford one is another issue.

An immigration lawyer can help someone facing deportation understand what their rights and options are.

DEPORTATION HEARINGS

If ICE interviews the detained immigrant and determines they want to go forward with deportation, the immigrant is given a Notice to Appear. This is essentially a court summons. The court process is overseen by the Executive Office for Immigration Review. In court, a judge who does not work for ICE will preside over the hearing to determine whether the immigrant should indeed be deported.

There are certain defenses an immigrant can use that may persuade the judge not to order deportation. Removal proceedings can take months or years, so often an undocumented immigrant isn't immediately deported. In fact, the only instances in which they are immediately deported are if a prior order of removal exists, if they sign a deportation agreement, or if they accept voluntary departure.

WHY SIGN A DEPORTATION AGREEMENT?

An immigrant facing deportation might opt to sign a deportation agreement rather than going through a hearing. If an immigrant is truly in the country without documentation and with no reasonable defense that might help win the right to stay, he or she might want to avoid the lengthy hearing and the fees associated with hiring an attorney. But an even more important consideration may be that signing a deportation agreement means that the immigrant will not have an order of deportation on their record. Getting a green card or applying for citizenship at a later date is much more difficult if an immigrant has an order of deportation from the Executive Office for Immigration Review on their record.

POSTING BOND

During the removal proceedings, if an immigrant is granted bond and can pay it, they may be released from custody and allowed to go about their life while waiting for the removal proceedings to be finished. It's essentially like a person accused of a crime being granted bail while waiting for trial. If the judge in a deportation hearing rules that the immigrant should be deported, then ICE carries out the removal order.

APPEALING A DEPORTATION RULING

One feature of the U.S. justice system is that court rulings can be appealed. If an immigrant feels they have good cause, they can contact the Administrative Appeals Office of U.S. Citizenship and Immigration Services to file an appeal. The Administrative Appeals Office will conduct a review of the appeal to ensure accuracy in the interpretation of immigration policy and law.

Immigrants ordered for deportation have the right to appeal the court's decision.

JUDGING AN APPEAL

The Administrative Appeals Office will usually provide what are called nonprecedent decisions. These decisions apply existing laws only to the case at hand. Occasionally, a nonprecedent decision can be adopted as later guidance for U.S. Citizenship and Immigration Services personnel, but usually it applies only to one specific case.

A recent example of such an adoption took place in early 2017. U.S. Citizenship and Immigration Services decided to adopt the decision that for matters of immigration policy, a "physician of national or international renown" could be defined as a doctor of medicine or osteopathy who is widely known and honored in the field of medicine in at least one country outside of the United States. This sort of adopted decision is useful when immigration courts are considering cases of immigrants with extraordinary ability. There is a specific type of visa for such immigrants, and having set guidance on the type of doctor who might qualify for that visa can be helpful.

Sometimes the Administrative Appeals Office will have the Attorney General review the case so that they can issue a precedent decision that will serve to provide guidance to legal personnel and the public when similar cases arise later.

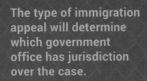

The type of immigration appeal will determine which government office has jurisdiction over the case.

I-881, Application for Suspension of Deportation or Special Rule Cancellation of Removal
(Pursuant to Section 203 of Public Law 105-100, NACARA)

CONTACTING THE RIGHT APPEALS OFFICE

The Administrative Appeals Office handles most immigration appeals cases, but not all. Certain cases fall under the jurisdiction of the Board of Immigration Appeals instead. These cases usually include cases where the immigrant has filed an application for relief from removal (such as those seeking asylum). They may also include cases where an immigrant has been excluded from applying for admission to the United States, or cases that involve petitioning to classify the status of immigrant relatives (for the purpose of gaining immigrant visas).

TYPES OF CASES

The Administrative Appeals Office hears appeals for more than 50 different types of immigration cases. These include the following:

- Employment-based immigrant and nonimmigrant visa petitions
- Immigrant petitions by entrepreneurs
- Applications for Temporary Protected Status
- Fiancé(e) petitions
- Applications for waivers based on inadmissibility
- Applications to reapply for admission after deportation
- Special immigrant visa petitions
- Orphan petitions
- T and U visa applications and petitions (these visas are for victims of human trafficking or other crimes)
- Applications to preserve residency for the purpose of naturalization
- ICE determinations regarding a breach of a surety bond

Refugees like these children from Syria may be eligible for Temporary Protected Status.

Filing an Appeal

Depending on the type of appeal, the immigrant can contact the relevant office and file the motion for appeal. If the Administrative Appeals Office handles the appeal, it will usually complete an initial field review of the case within 45 days. The full review is generally completed within six months.

Anyone filing an immigration appeal should seek legal advice. Hiring a lawyer can be expensive, so immigrants on low incomes can contact a nonprofit organization that will provide pro bono advice about immigration law and the appeals process. Immigration law is complex and thorny, and it is important to get things right. Anyone trying to navigate the system—especially immigrants with poor English skills—would be well served to take advantage of legal advice where available.

Applying for Readmission to the United States

If all appeals fail, an immigrant will be deported back to their country of citizenship. If they ever want to return to the United States, there are strict guidelines. These were set out in the Illegal Immigration Reform and Immigrant Responsibility Act of 1996. If an immigrant was illegally present in the United States for between 180 and 364 days, they must wait three years before they can be readmitted, unless they receive a pardon. If an immigrant was in the United States illegally for 365 days or more, they must wait ten years until they are eligible for readmission, unless they receive a waiver. If that immigrant tries to reenter the country illegally, then they are permanently barred from readmission.

If an immigrant is eligible for readmission after deportation, they can file Form I-212 (Application for Permission to Reapply for Admission into the United States After Deportation or Removal) through U.S. Citizenship and Immigration Services. They must also pay a fairly hefty fee to apply for readmission: as of December 2016, it was just under $1,000.

There is a part of the law, called Section 212(a)(9)(C), which states that an immigrant who has been deported and attempts to reenter the United States without being admitted will then be ineligible for reentry. If a deportee is deemed inadmissible under this clause, they cannot seek admission to the United States for at least ten years after their departure.

In San Diego in 2016, demonstrators protested policies that would potentially strip undocumented immigrants of their rights.

Leaving the Country

If an immigrant has no grounds to appeal a deportation order, they can request a Voluntary Departure. This means they can leave the United States on their own schedule (with some restrictions), but they must pay their own way. The

A Voluntary Departure leaves the door open for a possible return to the United States in the future.

benefit is that the immigrant will not have an order of deportation on their record, which may make it easier for them to apply for admission to the United States in the future. If an immigrant leaves on an order of deportation, that will stay on their record, but the government will pay for their transport back to their home country.

Unfortunately, deportation can sometimes be a swift and rather cold process, especially when deporting immigrants back to Mexico and Central America. Marta Chavez, a legal permanent resident, served time in prison for a drug charge. The day before she was due to be released from prison, ICE contacted her and asked to see her immigration paperwork. She didn't have the paperwork with her in prison, so ICE immediately put her on a bus to the Mexican border and dropped her off in Tijuana, with only $19 in her pocket.

JUSTIN MCNULTY

PERSONAL STORIES

Justin McNulty was born in England and when he was 12, his ailing mother sent him to stay with relatives in the United States. He had no problems until he tried to go to college, where they wanted proof of citizenship. Unable to provide it, Justin dropped out of college and worked as a DJ and a freelance illustrator.

After being in the country for about a decade, Justin applied for a green card but was denied and forced to sign voluntary deportation papers. He signed them but ignored them and went back to living under the radar in Los Angeles. Thirteen years later, immigration services caught up with him. They arrested him at his home, handcuffed him, and put him on a plane to a detention center in New Mexico.

He was kept in the detention center, which was little more than a prison, for three months. Eventually, he was transported back to England, with an order that he could not visit the United States for at least ten years. Justin has no family or friends in England. His life and any family he has are in the United States, yet he cannot visit them there for at least ten years.

Undocumented immigrants without proof of residency often find it easier to get freelance jobs, such as DJing.

CHAPTER 5

CURRENT IMMIGRATION LAWS

Today's immigration laws are far different from those established even as recently as the mid-twentieth century. As the makeup of our nation and our world shifts, no doubt immigration policies will continue to change. But for the moment, it's useful to understand the current immigration laws governing the United States.

LEGAL IMMIGRATION

U.S. immigration policy has four main goals: welcoming immigrants with skills that will benefit the economy, reuniting families, promoting diversity, and protecting refugees. Immigration law is incredibly complex, but there are some general principles and rules. For example, the number of immigrants allowed into the United States each year is limited to a certain number of people.

Exceptions are made when it's a case of a close family member joining one already residing in the United States. The government also allows noncitizens to come into the country on a temporary basis in some circumstances, such as students seeking an education at a U.S. university. A certain number of refugees are allowed in each year, too.

Immigrants entering the country can apply for a green card if they want to live and work permanently in the United States. (This excludes noncitizens such as students and refugees.) If their application is approved, the green card will allow them to legally remain in the United States. If they choose to, they can eventually apply for naturalization and the benefits and rights of full citizenship.

The quotas for immigrants coming to work are usually filled quickly.

IMMIGRATION FOR EMPLOYMENT

Immigrants coming to work in the United States can either get a temporary visa, or they can apply for a green card that will let them stay permanently. Only 140,000 immigrants per year can come to the United States for employment on a permanent basis, and this number includes family members. For example, a woman coming for an academic job might bring a husband and two young children. Only she will be working, but the family will count as four people out of that 140,000 limit.

IMMIGRATION FOR FAMILY MEMBERS

Immigration policy has favored keeping families together, so family-based immigration is one of the heaviest areas of immigration. In 2014, family-based immigrants made up 64 percent of all new permanent residents in the United States. However, even family-based immigration has limits. The number of visas issued per year for family members of permanent residents varies based on a complicated formula devised by Congress. It has generally been somewhere around half a million per year.

Some immigrant workers bring their families with them, while others hope to be reunited later.

THE DIVERSITY VISA PROGRAM

As part of the Immigration Act of 1990, Congress created a lottery called the Diversity Visa program. This is designed to allow entry to immigrants from countries that traditionally have had a low rate of immigration to the United States. Applicants to the program must come from countries that have sent fewer than 50,000 immigrants to the United States over the previous five years. Each year, visas are distributed randomly to 55,000 of these applicants to the Diversity Visa program.

There are a few other criteria applicants must meet. They must have a high-school education or its equivalent. They must also have worked for at least two years in some sort of profession that requires at least two years of training or experience. Further, that professional experience must have been earned within the past five years. An applicant's spouse and children can also apply.

Supporters of Obama's immigration policies gathered outside the Supreme Court in 2016.

IMMIGRATION FOR REFUGEES AND ASYLEES

For many years, refugees and asylees have also been welcome in the United States, assuming they can pass immigration screening and meet the criteria for immigration. A refugee is a person who flees from their home country to another country. Their home may be unsafe because of natural disaster or war. It may be unsafe because the individuals are being persecuted for religious or cultural beliefs. Whatever the reason, if the individual's home country is unsafe and they want to flee to another country, they can apply for refugee status.

Refugees are screened for entry based on numerous criteria, including whether they have family in the United States already and whether they are a member of a group thought to pose a threat to national security.

Asylees are slightly different because they generally are already living in the country where they want to establish residence. So, for example, if a person from a war-torn country is already living in the United States on a temporary basis, and they do not want to return to their home country, they can apply for asylum in the United States.

QUOTAS FOR REFUGEES AND ASYLEES

The number of refugees allowed into the United States each year is determined by the president and Congress. In 2016, the government agreed to admit a total of 85,000 refugees into the United States.

The government doesn't establish any specific quota for people granted asylum. The number is far lower than the number of refugees, though. For example, in 2014, there were 23,533 immigrants granted asylum.

People in refugee camps in the Middle East often anxiously await entry into a safe country, such as the United States.

CHAPTER 6

THE FUTURE OF IMMIGRATION

Given that the United States has long been a country of immigrants, it's a bit surprising how controversial the topic of immigration still is. Immigration was a key issue in the 2016 presidential race, with candidates Donald Trump and Hillary Clinton both highlighting their very different ideas on immigration issues and reform. Both candidates agreed that the United States's immigration system needed fixing, but they definitely didn't agree on the way to do it.

IMMIGRATION REFORM PROPOSALS

Although deportation rates were high during President Obama's administration, his immigration policies tended to favor giving immigrants a path to citizenship. Instead of just deporting all undocumented immigrants, he proposed amnesty programs that would allow long-term undocumented immigrants the chance to apply for citizenship.

Hillary Clinton, the Democratic nominee, generally followed Obama's vision. While acknowledging that there were problems in the current system, she spoke of a system of immigration reform that would provide a "pathway to full and equal citizenship." She saw this as having numerous benefits, including repairing broken immigrant families, making immigrants an official part of the United States economy, and strengthening national security.

The face of the United States—Mexico border is likely to change under the Trump administration.

However, Clinton did not win the election. She lost to Republican nominee Donald Trump, whose views on immigration were very different. Trump's proposal was to clamp down on immigration and rapidly deport undocumented immigrants, starting with those who had broken the law. He also promised to end the practice of undocumented immigrants working in the United States. Trump's most eye-catching suggestion was to build a physical wall along the entire length of the United States—Mexico border.

Immigrant Impact on the Job Market

One reason that many people are opposed to immigration is the idea that immigrants have a negative impact on the job market. There may never be enough jobs for every resident to earn a living, but sometimes unemployment rises to high levels. When this happens, people often begin to panic. This can color their view of immigrants.

If a person is out of work and sees an immigrant doing a job that he could be doing, that person might feel slighted. People often look for someone or something to blame when they're afraid. An unemployed person who is afraid he or she won't be able to provide for her family might choose to blame immigrants.

Unfair blame?

The author J.D. Vance grew up in a factory town in the American "Rust Belt." In 2016, he wrote a best-selling book called *Hillbilly Elegy*, which recounted his experiences working in a tile factory in a struggling town in the early 2000s. In it, he describes natural-born American citizens who would take factory jobs but then not put in much effort—or even just not bother to show up for work. Eventually, their employer would fire them. Vance wrote that some people reacted by blaming the government for allowing immigrants to take jobs. They refused to accept any responsibility for the role they may have played in their own job loss.

Vance was only describing what he saw at one factory, but he isn't the only one to make this characterization. In 2016, Amazon founder Jeff Bezos reportedly expressed frustration at the same phenomenon. He has been outspoken about his belief that a diverse immigrant workforce is a benefit to the U.S. economy.

There is no simple answer to what impact immigrants have on the overall unemployment rate. For every person who says that immigrants are taking jobs from U.S. citizens, you'll find another person who argues that immigrant labor actually helps stimulate the economy and create more jobs. It's likely that this argument will continue for years to come.

Impact on the Tax System

One major assumption some people make about undocumented immigrants is that they don't pay taxes. Some citizens assume that undocumented immigrants come to the United States, get a job that pays under the table, and pay no taxes. While this may be true in some instances, it is not universally true. In fact, 2016 reports stated that undocumented immigrants pay about $12 billion in taxes every year.

During Trump's 2016 campaign, he claimed that undocumented immigrants were getting $4.2 billion in tax credits every year. Naturally, that statement frustrated U.S. citizens who believed it to be true. However, it was later proven to be a misleading statement. It is also important to note that a report from the Institute on Taxation & Economic Policy (ITEP) showed that undocumented immigrants pay nearly $12 billion in state and local taxes a year. According to the *New York Times*, Trump himself may have actually avoided paying federal income tax for a number of years, due to certain tax rules.

 Some people find it interesting that immigrants may pay more into the U.S. tax system than President Trump may have in recent years.

IMMIGRANT TAXPAYERS

According to ITEP, at least 50 percent of undocumented immigrants file tax returns. And even the ones who don't file often have taxes deducted from their paychecks. If this is the case, they may not be paying exactly the correct amount, but they're still paying something. Some of them may actually be overpaying—many people find when they file their tax returns that they actually overpaid, and they get a nice refund check back. Undocumented immigrants who don't file a return can't claim a refund.

TAX REVENUES FROM UNDOCUMENTED IMMIGRANTS

Undocumented immigrants reportedly pay about $11.64 billion in taxes each year: $6.9 billion in sales and excise taxes, $3.6 billion in property taxes, and $1.1 billion in personal income tax.

SOCIAL SECURITY

Undocumented immigrants also pay into Social Security, even though they may never benefit from it. U.S. citizens are entitled to Social Security benefits when they reach a qualifying age, but many of the undocumented immigrants who pay into that system and will never become naturalized citizens, so they won't be able to claim benefits.

For some immigrants, paying into this system isn't exactly by choice. To get a job, many undocumented immigrants will purchase a fake Social Security card, because a valid Social Security number is required for employment. Employers may not realize the cards are fake—some don't really check, or pay close enough attention. These employers submit the number on a W-2 form for that employee, along with a tax payment. If the federal government finds the Social Security number isn't linked to anyone they have on file when they receive the payment, they simply put the money in a fund called the Earnings Suspense File. Eventually, a large chunk of that money goes to pay out Social Security benefits to U.S. citizens.

WHAT IMMIGRANTS PUT INTO THE SYSTEM

This is actually what happens for a fairly significant number of undocumented immigrants. Stephen Goss, the chief actuary of the Social Security Administration, reported that in 2010, an estimated 1.8 million immigrants were working under fake or stolen Social Security cards. He estimated that by 2040 that number will be close to 3.4 million.

Goss also calculated that in 2010 undocumented immigrants paid $13 billion into the Social Security system. In other words, undocumented immigrants weren't draining the system; they were actually adding to it.

 Immigrants—both documented and undocumented—are a vital part of California's agricultural economy.

CHANGING THE RULES

One attempt to curtail the hiring of undocumented immigrants ended up resulting in more tax revenue. The Immigration Reform and Control Act was passed in 1986. It made it illegal for employers to knowingly hire unauthorized immigrants. However, the unauthorized immigrants in the U.S. still wanted to work, so a market for fake Social Security cards, birth certificates, and other forms of ID sprang up. Undocumented immigrants who had previously just worked under the table and paid no taxes ended up getting fake documentation and paying into the tax system. The government's goal of curbing the hiring of undocumented immigrants ended up backfiring—but it did create a significant revenue stream.

THE ITIN SYSTEM

In 1996, the government instituted the ITIN (Individual Taxpayer Identification Number) program. Under this program, a person who cannot obtain a valid Social Security number can instead be issued an ITIN that they can use to file taxes. The ITIN program has brought in more revenue for the government. In 2010, about 3 million people used an ITIN to pay more than $870 million in income taxes.

Federal tax laws say that the Internal Revenue Service cannot share data with the Department of Homeland Security, which means that even if undocumented immigrants have an ITIN, it cannot be used to identify and subsequently deport them. It is only used for tax purposes. However, it can eventually be used to help an immigrant obtain citizenship, because a history of paying taxes can help an immigrant prove a desire to obtain legal residency status.

IMMIGRANT IMPACT ON NATIONAL SECURITY

National security has become a frequent talking point since the terrorist attacks of September 11, 2001, that killed thousands of people. Since that tragic day, some Americans have felt less safe in the United States, and have become suspicious of foreign-born people, specifically those of Middle Eastern descent.

The September 11th attacks were carried out by al-Qaeda, a radical Islamist group, and another radical Islamist group, ISIS, is currently carrying out attacks around the world. But even so, many citizens rightly point out that not every Muslim is a threat. Just as there are many branches of Christianity, there are many branches of Islam—and only a very small number of practicing Muslims belong to the radical branches.

Nearly 3,000 people were killed in the September 11 attacks, including many immigrants.

WORTH THE RISK?

Some Americans believe that the best way to keep the country safe is not to admit any Muslims at all into the United States. They feel that it's just not worth the risk, because any Muslim could potentially belong to a radical branch and could be plotting a terrorist attack. But that could be said of practically anyone. In fact, any citizen of any faith—immigrant or not—could become radicalized or join a terrorist group at any time.

The 2013 Boston Marathon attacks are proof of that. Brothers Tamerlan and Dzhokhar Tsarnaev planted bombs near the end of the marathon's course that ultimately killed three people and injured 264 others. Both brothers were immigrants. Tamerlan had a green card and his application for U.S. citizenship was in progress at the time of the attacks. His brother Dzhokhar had become a naturalized U.S. citizen on September 11, 2012, just 7 months before the bombings. The brothers had apparently become followers of radical Islam after coming to the United States.

The 2013 Boston Marathon attacks terrified local residents, as well as people across the country.

Trump's solution

During the 2016 presidential campaign, Donald Trump proposed a temporary ban on Muslims entering the United States, as well as a registry for all Muslims living in the United States. He saw this as a way to prevent further radical Islamist attacks. To some Americans, this sounded like a good solution. To others, it seemed eerily similar to the Jewish registry that Adolf Hitler established before World War II, and the ban on Asian immigrants in the nineteenth century.

Shortly after taking office in January 2017, Trump began putting his plans in action. During his first week in office, he signed executive orders to begin construction of the border wall with Mexico, as well as to begin deporting the approximately 11 million undocumented immigrants living in the United States back to their home countries.

Trump's executive orders also blocked all Syrian refugees from entering the United States indefinitely, in case they turned out to be followers of radical Islam. These also barred all refugees—from any country—from entering the United States for at least 120 days, and suspended immigration from several predominantly-Muslim countries. However, these executive orders were blocked by the courts, causing a legal battle. Trump also immediately ordered the hiring of another 5,000 Border Patrol agents and 10,000 immigration officers.

THE RIGHT SOLUTION?

Defending his deportation orders, Trump said, "We are going to get the bad ones out—the criminals and the drug dealers and gangs and gang members...The day is over when they can stay in our country and wreak havoc. We are going to get them out, and we are going to get them out fast." But while most U.S. citizens would indeed be happy to have "the bad ones" leave, the concern is that immigrants who have not committed violent crimes or aggravated felonies will be deported as well.

Trump's orders specify that immigrants who are priorities for deportation include "those who have engaged in fraud or willful misrepresentation in connection with any official matter or application before a governmental agency." And while fraud may sound like a serious crime, the wording of the order makes it so that even an undocumented immigrant who has signed an employment contract to work in the United States (and contributes to the tax system) is subject to deportation.

SANCTUARY CITIES

There are dozens of cities in the United States designated as "sanctuary cities." In these cities, local authorities limit their cooperation with federal authorities who are looking to detain undocumented immigrants. But Trump's order threatens the sanctuary cities with losing federal grant money if they continue to limit their cooperation.

Joanne Lin of the American Civil Liberties Union explained why her organization was concerned by Trump's plans: "They're setting out to unleash this deportation force on steroids, and local police will be able to run wild, so we're tremendously concerned about the impact that could have on immigrants and families across the country...The fear quotient is going to go up exponentially."

At the 2016 Republican National Convention, demonstrators protested against Trump's proposed immigration policies.

Nancy Pelosi, the Democratic Minority Leader in the U.S. House of Representatives, expressed similar frustration with the plan. She said, "The president is turning his back on both our history and our values as a proud nation of immigrants….Punishing cities that do not want their local police forces forced to serve as President Trump's deportation dragnet does nothing to fix our immigration system or keep Americans safe."

WHAT'S NEXT?

The future of immigration and deportation is unknown. Those who support President Trump's immigration plans feel that his actions are the first steps toward strengthening national security and protecting American citizens' safety and jobs. Those who oppose his plans feel as if they will destroy the very foundation on which the United States was created. Only time will tell.

GLOSSARY

aggravated felony Criminal offense that carries severe consequences.

amnesty Official pardon for someone.

asylee A person seeking or granted political asylum.

Bracero Program A series of laws under which Mexican citizens could work in the United States.

crimes of moral turpitude Crimes that shock the public conscience, such as murder, kidnapping, robbery, and aggravated assault.

forced labor Work that people are forced to do under the threat of punishment.

Great Depression A deep economic downturn from 1929 to 1939.

indentured servitude Being contractually bound to work for another person for a set period of time to pay off a debt.

Internal Revenue Service Federal agency responsible for collecting taxes.

Meiji Restoration Japan's return to imperial rule in 1868.

Miranda rights A statement about the rights of a person being arrested.

naturalization Admittance of a person to the citizenship of another country.

nonprecedent decisions Legal decisions that apply only to a particular case and do not provide guidance for future legal decisions.

osteopathy A branch of medicine that focuses on manipulating the bones, muscles, and joints.

pardon A remission of the legal consequences of a conviction.

precedent decisions Legal decisions that set the precedent for future legal decisions.

pro bono Work done without charge to a client.

refugee A person forced to leave their home country to escape persecution, natural disaster, or political unrest.

repatriation campaigns Campaigns designed to encourage immigrants to voluntarily return to their home country.

Social Security A social insurance program that covers retirement, disability, and survivors' benefits.

surety bond Assurance by an individual that he or she will take responsibility for another person's actions.

xenophobia Fear or hatred of people from other countries.

FOR MORE INFORMATION

BOOKS

Burgan, Michael. *Ellis Island: An Interactive History Adventure*. North Mankato, MN: Capstone Press, 2013.

Currie, Stephen. *Undocumented Immigrant Youth*. San Diego, CA: ReferencePoint Press, 2016.

Grande, Reyna. *The Distance Between Us*. New York, NY: Aladdin, 2016.

McCormick, Lisa Wade. *Frequently Asked Questions About Growing Up as an Undocumented Immigrant*. New York, NY: The Rosen Publishing Group, 2013.

WEBSITES

Find out more about immigration at the U.S. Citizenship and Immigration Services:
www.uscis.gov

Justia provides an overview of immigration law and links to other immigration law resources:
www.justia.com/immigration

Visit this website for an overview of the U.S. court system:
www.dummies.com/education/politics-government/ getting-to-know-the-u-s-court-systems

Publisher's note to educators and parents: Our editors have carefully reviewed these websites to ensure that they are suitable for students. Many websites change frequently, however, and we cannot guarantee that a site's future contents will continue to meet our high standards of quality and educational value. Be advised that students should be closely supervised whenever they access the Internet.

INDEX